Ohio
The Buckeye State

Marcia Amidon Lusted

PowerKiDS
press™

New York

For my son Nick, with love

Published in 2010 by The Rosen Publishing Group, Inc.
29 East 21st Street, New York, NY 10010

First Edition

Editor: Nicole Pristash
Book Design: Greg Tucker
Photo Researcher: Jessica Gerweck

Photo Credits: Cover, pp. 5, 19, 22 (bird), 22 (flower) Shutterstock.com; p. 7 © Richard A. Cooke/ Corbis; p. 9 © North Wind/North Wind Picture Archives; p. 11 © Jeff Greenberg/age fotostock; p. 13 www.istockphoto.com/Paul Tessier; pp. 15, 22 (famous people) Getty Images; p. 17 © Superstock, Inc; p. 22 (tree) Courtesy of Wikimedia Commons; p. 22 (animal) © www.istockphoto.com/ MidwestWilderness.

Library of Congress Cataloging-in-Publication Data

Lusted, Marcia Amidon.
  Ohio : the Buckeye State / Marcia Amidon Lusted. — 1st ed.
      p. cm. — (Our amazing states)
  Includes index.
  ISBN 978-1-4042-8122-6 (library binding) — ISBN 978-1-4358-3370-8 (pbk.) —
ISBN 978-1-4358-3371-5 (6-pack)
  1. Ohio—Juvenile literature. I. Title.
  F491.3.L876 2010
  977.1—dc22
                                                2009004853

Manufactured in the United States of America

Contents

The Great State of Ohio

There is a state where you can see a giant Indian mound shaped like a snake. In this state, you can visit an **amusement park** that has 17 roller coasters. Which state is this? It is Ohio!

Ohio is found in the midwestern part of the United States. The top of the state borders Lake Erie. The Ohio River runs along the bottom of the state on the borders of Kentucky and West Virginia.

Ohio is known for its factories, which once attracted **immigrants** from all over the world. Along with Virginia, Ohio is known as the mother of presidents because seven U.S. presidents were born in Ohio.

Cleveland, shown here, is one of the most populated cities in Ohio. About 478,403 people make this city their home.

The Mound Builders

The name Ohio comes from an Iroquois word that means "great water." The Iroquois are a Native American **tribe**. They first gave this nickname to the Ohio River.

Native Americans lived in Ohio for thousands of years before the Europeans came. Some Native Americans began building dirt mounds 3,000 years ago. These mounds were used as **forts**, as places for **ceremonies**, and as places to bury the dead. Many of these mounds can still be seen today. Later tribes, such as the Shawnee, grew crops and hunted deer in the area. Many of these tribes would later help French settlers fight the British.

This is the Great Serpent Mound, near Peebles. The mound is about ¼ mile (.4 km) long and around 3 feet (1 m) high.

Exploration and War

Around 1670, a French **explorer** named René-Robert Cavelier de La Salle was the first European to explore the land that now includes Ohio. He claimed the area for France. However, British settlers claimed it, too. They wanted to settle there and trade with the Native Americans.

The French went to war with the British over who would control the land. This was known as the French and Indian War. The British won in 1763, and they claimed the area. After the British lost the **American Revolution**, though, the United States took control of all British land. Ohio became the seventeenth state in 1803.

This image shows René-Robert Cavelier de La Salle (standing) and his men exploring in their boat. La Salle was the first European to see the Ohio River.

Lakes and Plains

For those traveling, Ohio is easy to cross. Ohio has no mountains or deserts to make traveling hard. Instead, most of the state is rolling plains. There are some hills and deep valleys, though, on the Allegheny **Plateau** in eastern Ohio.

Lake Erie, one of the Great Lakes, serves as a place for ships to travel and bring goods to the Midwest. Ohio was once covered with forest, but early settlers cut many of the trees down and used them for building.

In Ohio, summer is often warm, and winter can be very cold. Northern Ohio gets more than 2 feet (61 cm) of snow every winter.

Many people swim in Lake Erie during the summer months. These children are swimming in the lake in Cleveland's Edgewater Park.

The Buckeye State

Ohio is home to many plants and animals. The state gets its nickname, the Buckeye State, from a tree called the buckeye that is common in Ohio. The nuts of this tree look like a buck's eye. A buck is another name for an adult male deer. Other types of trees and plants, such as maples, hickories, and ferns, grow in Ohio's forests. Yellow and brown flowers called black-eyed Susans can be seen along Ohio's roadsides.

White-tailed deer, black bears, and foxes live in Ohio's woodlands. Wildlife is also found in Ohio's cities. Bats, squirrels, and raccoons can sometimes be found living in people's homes!

Unlike female white-tailed deer, bucks have antlers. Antlers are large, branchlike horns that grow on the tops of their heads.

What's Made in Ohio?

Because of Ohio's flat plains, there are many farms there. However, Ohio is known for the **products** that are made in its factories. Akron is called the Rubber Capital of the World because several tire companies have been based there. Cincinnati is home to Procter & Gamble, a company that makes soap and other household products.

Ohio makes more cars than any other state except Michigan. Ohio factories put together cars, and they also make car parts, such as **engines**.

There are many mines in Ohio. Coal, natural gas, and oil are mined throughout the state. There are also mines that produce salt!

This car is being built at a GM car factory in Lordstown, Ohio. This factory has been building cars since 1966.

A Visit to Columbus

Columbus is Ohio's capital city. More than 711,470 people live there, making it the largest city in the state. Most people in Columbus come from European backgrounds. Some are Hispanic, or Latino. Other people have moved there from Vietnam and Russia.

There are many historic places to visit in Columbus. The state capitol was finished in 1861. Ohio Village is a **replica** of a village from the time of the Civil War. German Village has brick homes from the nineteenth century. For fun, people visit COSI, a science **museum**, the Columbus Zoo, and the Franklin Park Conservatory, where many interesting plants can be seen.

The Ohio statehouse, Ohio's capitol, is one of the oldest working statehouses in America. Building started in 1839, and it took 22 years to finish.

17

The Roller Coaster Capital

Many people from around the country travel to Ohio to visit Cedar Point Amusement Park, in Sandusky. The park has 17 roller coasters, more than any other park in the world! Because of this, the park is called the Roller Coaster Capital of the World. More than three million people visit the park every year, making it one of Ohio's biggest **tourist attractions**.

Cedar Point has four areas that are just for kids, as well as an area called Soak City. Soak City has water rides to cool people off on hot days. The park also has places to hear music and see shows. There is something for everyone at Cedar Point!

The Blue Streak is the longest-running roller coaster at Cedar Point. It was built in 1964.

Come to Ohio

Ohio has many things to offer. You can visit the Rock and Roll Hall of Fame, in Cleveland, which honors rock bands and singers. The National Museum of the United States Air Force, near Dayton, is another fun place to see. This museum displays hundreds of aircraft and other objects used by the Air Force.

If you would rather be outside, you can enjoy the shorefront along Lake Erie. If you are looking for history, you can visit the old Native American mound that is shaped like a snake.

No matter what you like, Ohio has many reasons for you to come visit. Maybe you will even want to stay!

Glossary

American Revolution (uh-MER-uh-ken reh-vuh-LOO-shun) Battles that soldiers from the colonies fought against Britain for freedom, from 1775 to 1783.

amusement park (uh-MYOOZ-ment PAHRK) A place where people pay to go on rides.

ceremonies (SER-ih-moh-neez) Special actions done at certain moments.

engines (EN-jinz) Machines inside cars or airplanes that make the cars or airplanes move.

explorer (ek-SPLOR-er) A person who travels and looks for new land.

forts (FORTS) Strong buildings or places that can be guarded against enemies.

immigrants (IH-muh-grunts) People who moved to a new country from another country.

museum (myoo-ZEE-um) A place where art or historical or scientific objects are kept for people to see.

plateau (pla-TOH) A wide, flat, high piece of land.

products (PRAH-dukts) Things that are produced.

replica (REH-plih-kuh) A copy of an object used in the past, such as a building.

tourist attractions (TUHR-ist uh-TRAK-shunz) Places that people from out of town visit.

tribe (TRYB) A group of people who share the same way of living, language, and relatives.

Ohio State Symbols

**State Tree
Buckeye**

**State Animal
White-Tailed
Deer**

State Flag

**State Bird
Cardinal**

**State Flower
Scarlet Carnation**

State Seal

Famous People from Ohio

Ulysses S. Grant
(1822–1885)
Born in
Point Pleasant, OH
U.S. President

Annie Oakley
(1860–1926)
Born in Darke County, OH
Sharpshooter/Entertainer

Wilbur Wright
(1867–1912)
Orville Wright
(1871–1948)
Born in Dayton, OH
Inventors

Ohio State Map

Legend

○ Major City

★ Capital

〜 River

Ohio State Facts

Area: 41,222 square miles (106,764 sq km)

Population: About 11,353,140

Motto: "With God, all things are possible"

State Song: "Beautiful Ohio," music by Mary Earl, words by Ballard MacDonald and Wilbert McBride

Index

Web Sites

Due to the changing nature of Internet links, PowerKids Press has developed an online list of Web sites related to the subject of this book. This site is updated regularly. Please use this link to access the list:

www.powerkidslinks.com/amst/oh/